DISCARDED BY
URBANA FREE LIBRARY

The Urbana Free Library

To renew: call **217-367-4057**
or go to **urbanafreelibrary.org**
and select **My Account**

The Rotary Club of Urbana is pleased
to donate this book to the
Urbana Free Library in honor of:

NAVID'S STORY

A Real-Life Account of His Journey from Iran

Editor: Michelle Hasselius
Production Specialist: Tori Abraham
The illustrations in this book were created digitally.

Picture Window Books are published by Capstone,
1710 Roe Crest Drive, North Mankato, Minnesota 56003
www.mycapstone.com

Copyright © 2018 by Picture Window Books, a Capstone
imprint. All rights reserved. No part of this publication may be
reproduced in whole or in part, or stored in a retrieval system,
or transmitted in any form or by any means, electronic,
mechanical, photocopying, recording, or otherwise, without
written permission of the publisher.

Library of Congress Cataloging-in-Publication Data
Library of Congress Cataloging-in-Publication data is
available on the Library of Congress website.
ISBN 978-1-5158-1415-3 (library binding)
ISBN 978-1-5158-1421-4 (eBook PDF)

Glossary

border (BOR-dur)—the dividing line between a country or region and another

cottage (KOT-ij)—a small house, especially in a beach or country setting

execute (EK-suh-kyoot)—to kill someone as punishment

Kurd (KERD)—a member of a group of people who live in a region that include parts of Turkey, Iran, and Iraq

refugee (ref-yuh-JEE)—a person forced to flee his or her home because of war or other disasters

NAVID'S STORY

A Real-Life Account of His Journey from Iran

by Andy Glynne

illustrated by Jonathan Topf

PICTURE WINDOW BOOKS

a capstone imprint

My name is Navid. This is the story of my journey from Iran.

We left Iran because my dad disagreed with the government. I remember government officials visited us one day. My dad's life was in danger. He had to leave the country immediately.

Many people who were against
the Iranian government have
similar stories.

I suppose my dad was lucky. Members of my mom's family were executed because they were Kurdish.

After my dad left, the officials kept coming back to our house. They would ask my mom where he had gone. We decided we had to leave too.

I remember everyone was really
sad the night we left Iran.

At first I didn't understand why they were
sad. But when I got to the airport, I realized
I was leaving my country for good. I was
upset for almost the whole journey.

We flew to Italy. From there we traveled mainly on foot.
We had to jump over a high wire fence. It was really scary.

We walked through a forest at night and were stopped by police. The sound of the police dog barking was terrifying.

I remember staying in
a cottage one night.
I think it was in Slovenia,
but I'm not sure.

The next night
we had to leave
the cottage. I was
scared, because I
could see the concern
on my mom's face.

We climbed into the back of a truck in France.

It was dark and uncomfortable.

I felt scared and really wanted to get out.

We finally arrived in our new country. Then
I remember someone used a knife to cut
open the cover on the back of the truck.

It was just like in the movies. The sunlight flooded in to show my mom and me sitting in the back of the truck.

When we got out of the truck, the border officials questioned us. But they were really friendly.

That was the day I saw my dad for the first time in years.

It was the weirdest thing.
It wasn't what I expected at all.

At first I didn't recognize him.
Then he explained he was my dad,
and he had missed me so much.

I remember sitting in the back of the car.
My mom and dad were in the front.

It was nighttime. I spent the whole journey looking at him.
I was trying to figure out who he was and what was happening.

Soon I was more comfortable around him. I figured out
that he really was my dad!

I started school in my new country. The first few days were really hard. Not because of the other students or teachers. But because I didn't know anything—not even the language.

I felt like an outsider. That was really scary for me.

One memory I have from school was when my mom came to talk to me at recess. We had to talk through the fence.

When the school bell rang, my mom had to go home.
I held on to the fence like I was in some sort of prison.

I couldn't understand
much of what was
said to me at school.
I felt very lonely.

People looked friendly. But it was scary that I didn't know what they were saying.

School was difficult for me at first.

I had to learn how to do everything.

At my school there were lots of kids
from different backgrounds.

There were other refugee kids at my school.
After school we met at a center for kids in
similar situations.

We could share our experiences. It was helpful for me to talk with other kids.

Even though the first few months were difficult, having that sense of support was amazing for me. And of course, I had my mom and dad.